WOLVERHAMPTON SPORTING HEROES

WOLVERHAMPTON SPORTING HEROES

JOEY BREW

First published 2010

Amberley Publishing Plc
Cirencester Road, Chalford,
Stroud, Gloucestershire, GL6 8PE

www.amberley-books.com

British Library Cataloguing in Publication Data.
A catalogue record for this book is available from the British Library.

ISBN 978 1 84868 485 0

Typesetting and Origination by FONTHILLDESIGN.
Printed in Great Britain.

CONTENTS

ACKNOWLEDGEMENTS

I have to thank many people for the help they have given me in compiling this book, but most of all my Dad, Alec, who, after having published over thirty books of his own, was able to guide me through the process and pass on his accumulated knowledge of the city's sporting history. Everyone I have spoken to has been unfailingly willing to go out of their way to assist and to expand my knowledge of 'their' sport and 'their' club. At my own club, Wolverhampton Cricket Club, I was aided by David Barnes and David Lycett. I hope the book will be successful, so that I might in a small way repay some of the wonderful help and experiences I have enjoyed at Danescourt over the last ten years. Elsewhere, and in no particular order, there was Club Historian Graham Hughes, and Simon Pagett at Wolverhampton Wanderers, Mac Abbotts and Bill Kelly at Wolverhampton Judo Club, Alan Cooper, Ron Aspey, and Ted Williams at Wolverhampton Wheelers, Ken Evans and Dave Guest at Wolverhampton & Bilston Athletics Club, Chris van Straaten and Ty Wooffenden at Wolverhampton Wolves Speedway Team, Ken Dolman and John Thomas at Wolverhampton Amateur Boxing Club, Colin Hole at Wolverhampton Lawn Tennis & Squash Club, and at my own tennis club, Albert Lawn Tennis Club, Tom Hole, Alan Spencer and Bob Fearn. I also have to thank the late Jim Boulton, Ray Jones, Dave Hill, and Honorary Alderman Doreen Seiboth.

EXPLANATIONS

The City of Wolverhampton is blessed with a number of famous sports clubs, which have brought national and international glory to the town, most famously Wolverhampton Wanderers, the one reason, more than any other, that the city's name is known throughout the world. Arguably, though, the Wolves are not the most successful local sports club in the city, Wolverhampton & Bilston Athletics Club and Wolverhampton Judo Club can both lay claim to that honour, having each produced countless international and national champions, and dominating, for a period, the club competitions in their sports.

Most of the clubs representing other sports may not have ever been national champions in the same way but have still produced individual champions of national and international renown. One such institution is Wolverhampton Cricket Club, the oldest sports club in the city, which has often achieved glory at the level at which it competes, most recently in the Birmingham League, and has produced individual cricketers who have gone on to play for major counties, and even England. The club fields five adult teams each Saturday, and two each Sunday, and recruits this large playing staff largely from its own junior ranks.

Each year, the club fields seven junior teams, one for every age group from Under 10 to Under 16 from a junior membership of over 120, and scores of those boys and girls represent their counties, usually Staffordshire or Shropshire, each summer. The junior teams regularly reach the latter stages of the national Under 13 and Under 15 championships and dominate Staffordshire and West Midlands competitions. This production line of talent has been overseen for many years by Arthur Pickering and his team of dedicated coaches on the attractive surroundings of the two pitches at Danescourt, Tettenhall, but for over a century, the club operated from an increasingly dilapidated wooden pavilion. In 2008, a brand-new, state-of-the-art pavilion was completed, but fund-raising activities to pay for this marvellous new facility still continue. The proceeds from this book will go towards the Pavilion Fund.

Firstly, I have to define what I mean by the term Wolverhampton Sporting Heroes. It does not necessarily mean born in Wolverhampton, for no one could deny that Billy Wright is one of the greatest of all the city's sporting icons, but he was born in Ironbridge in Shropshire; yet Arthur Rowley, who was born in Wolverhampton, and went on to become the Football League's all-time leading goalscorer, never played for the Wolves, except as a guest in eight wartime games. Tessa Sanderson, who brought Olympic golden glory to Wolverhampton, was actually born in Kingston, Jamaica, but Sam Doble, born in the town centre, and who played for England's rugby team and broke the record for the most club points scored in a season, played for Moseley in Birmingham, not a local club.

The criteria for inclusion in the book is thus twofold: the teams and individuals who have represented clubs in the town and have gone on to achieve national and international renown, whether they were born in Wolverhampton or not, and secondly, those who were born in the town, but may have plied their skills and achieved sporting fame elsewhere. Even so, I have had to be selective in the names I have chosen to highlight. I could have filled the book, quite easily, with footballers, or even athletes, but that would have been unfair on other sports. It might be that I have omitted someone who is a hero to many in the town, particularly if it were in an unlikely sport. If there are champion yachtsmen or mountaineers born in Wolverhampton, for instance, I hope I can be forgiven for overlooking them, in a town far from the sea, or indeed a mountain. If your own sporting hero is missing from the book, please forgive me.

The old wooden pavilion at Wolverhampton Cricket Club, Danescourt Road, Tettenhall, which served for over a century, photographed on the day of its last use for a cricket match. This pavilion has hosted many famous cricketers, such as W. G. Grace, Alan Donald, and the club's own Rachel Heyhoe-Flint and Vikram Solanki. The proceeds of this book will help finance the magnificent replacement pavilion, which stands on the spot today.

Opposite: The Penn Cricket Club side, which won the 1957 *Express & Star* Trophy, at their Mount Road ground. They were to win another *Express & Star* Knockout Cup in 1975. The club had particular success in the 1990s, winning the Staffordshire Division One Championship four times and the Knockout Cup eight times out of ten. This period resulted in them being promoted to the Birmingham League, the top of the new national club cricket pyramid, and they won the Division Two title at their first attempt, in 1999, without losing a match. The wooden buildings, which can be seen in the background of this picture, were replaced by a brick pavilion in the early 1960s.

CRICKET

The oldest sporting club in Wolverhampton is Wolverhampton Cricket Club, which was founded in 1835 and is the premier cricket club of the area, boasting a huge array of junior teams, which have churned out talent such as Vikram Solanki and Georgia Elwiss. The club played on various grounds until alighting at its present site at Danescourt in 1890. It came into its own after the Second World War, and came to dominate local cricket, winning the Midlands Club Championship seven times during the 1970s. In 1989, the club joined the Birmingham League, one of the top club competitions in the country. The Birmingham & District Premier League, which was founded in 1888, is the oldest club league in the world, and Wolverhampton won it in only their second season, 1990, and won it again in 1998, coming second in 2009.

The junior teams have won too many honours to list. For instance, the Under 13s have been Staffs County Champions nineteen times since 1987, West Midland League Champions eleven times, East Shropshire League winners eight times, West Midland KO Cup winners fourteen times, and National Under 13 finalists twelve times, finally winning the national title in 2009. The Under 15s have been Staffs Cup winners thirteen times, West Midland Cup winners nine times, and National finalists five times. The Under 9s, Under 11s and Under 16s have similar lists of honours, a tribute, in particular, to Arthur Pickering, in charge of the junior section and his team of coaches.

Penn Cricket Club is the other 'Centenary' Club playing cricket in Wolverhampton, having been founded in 1908. They started playing on Penn Common and only moved to their present ground in Mount Road in 1935, and now play in the Birmingham League. Other notable clubs in the area include Old Wulfrunians and Tettenhall, Wightwick & Finchfield, and Fordhouses.

W. G. Grace and G. L. Jessop pose with the other players in a match between a Mr G. L. Jessop's XI and a Mr H. D. Stratton's XI, played at Tettenhall. From right to left, top row: Umpire, P. S. Bayliss, J. A. Healing, W. C. Hands, A. B. Crawford, Grimshaw, Charlesworth, Alleston, C. B. Grace, Dennet, W. J. Hodgkinson, Datton (umpire). Second row: P. Healing, A. C. Finnis, Revd E. M. Baker, H. D. Stratton, W. G. Grace, G. L. Jessop, Sir Cecil Moon, C. P. Blewitt. Third row: H. Hextall, E. W. Page, W. W. Odell, W. J. Beddows. Jessop's won by 26 runs in the two-day, two-innings match, which was played on 21 and 22 July 1911. Grace is the most famous player of his era and his line upon once getting out cheaply – 'They've come to see me bat, not you bowl, son' – has gone down in cricketing folklore. Jessop was renowned as a fast-scoring batsman, hitting a number of centuries in less than an hour. Grace was out cheaply in both innings here, but did take two wickets with the ball, while Jessop made 49 and 30 and took the last wicket to win the match. The match winners for Jessop's XI were Alleston, who made 51 and 118, and Dennet, who took ten wickets. Odell was the star man for Stratton's, scoring 95 and taking nine wickets. H. D. Stratton was the captain of Wolverhampton Cricket Club from 1882 to 1911, so this match may not be unconnected with his retirement.

Rachel Heyhoe-Flint, OBE, was an England cricketer who represented her country for twenty-two years, and was captain for twelve of them. Heyhoe-Flint was born in Wolverhampton and has been a director of Wolverhampton Wanderers FC since 1997. She played 22 Tests and 23 ODIs for England, and once held the world record for the highest Test score, a mammoth 179 against Australia. She also played hockey for England, in goal, and played both netball and golf for Staffordshire.

The 1st XI of Wolverhampton Cricket Club in 1960. From left to right, top row: D. Rossi, D. H. Koates, R. C. Davies, R. H. Bulley, D. J. Barnes, A. J. Claxton. Bottom row: A. P. Wilkes, R. V. Lawry, A. W. U. Norgrove, J. K. Sadler, J. Robbins.

The county players of Wolverhampton Cricket Club one year, from junior to senior and veteran. Left to right, top row: M. Hampton, P. Tomlinson, V. Solanki (Under 13), A. Mackelworth, A. Chapman (Minor Counties), S. Griffiths (Under 19), P. Griffiths (Under 13). Middle row: G. Lunn, D. Barnes, A. Orton, P. Jones, D. Lowe (Over 50). Bottom row: S. Lycett, J. Singh, G. Franklin (Under 11). Simon Lycett is now the first team captain and led the First XI to second place in the Birmingham Premier League in 2009. David Barnes is currently club president.

The National Club Knockout finalists of 1988, Wolverhampton CC, at Lords. From left to right, top row: A. McLeish (scorer), M. Yates, R. Griffin, T. Heap, D. Lampitt, J. Turner, C. Horton, A. McKinlay, G.Williams, M. Stanley, K. Sadley. Bottom row: P. Evans (chairman), D. Manning, D. Barnes, P. Jones (capt.), R. Wood (vice capt.), J. Hughes, S. Patel. The match was played at Edgbaston after bad weather ruined the day at Lords, and Enfield were easily triumphant, winning by nine wickets. Nevertheless, Wolverhampton won this prestigious trophy in 1973 and again in 1999.

The U13 Midshires winners of 1988, one of twelve times they won this title, and here featuring a future England player in Vikram Solanki. From left to right, top row: I. O'Sullivan, V. Solanki, J. Reynolds, P. Tomlinson. Bottom row: S. Griffiths, G. Onions, S. Paul, P. Griffiths. Born and raised in Wolverhampton, Solanki went on to enjoy an England career, playing for the one-day team 51 times. He made his Worcestershire debut in 1993; he is about to embark on his eighteenth season and sixth as captain. Solanki scored two centuries and five half-centuries for England but never established himself as a regular, and despite many appearances for the England 'A' team, he never made his Test debut.

The Wolverhampton side that won the South Staffs Sunday League Division Two in 2004, including current England U21 cricketer Georgia Elwiss. From right to left, top row: P. Porter (umpire), D. Woollatt, J. Athawal, G. Elwiss, J. Banks, L. Smith (scorer). Bottom row: Z. Khan, A. Kataria, A. J. Smith, J. Crowe (capt.), N. Vaidya, J. Kholi, L. Elwiss (Georgia's brother and, like her, a Staffordshire County junior player). David Woollatt was Staffordshire Young Bowler of the Year that year, and Adam Smith was Young Batsman.

Wolverhampton's National U-13 Club Champions in 2009, at the annual finals at Oakham School. Left to right, back row: Arthur Pickering (the architect of the club's massive success at junior level), Jack Biddulph (assistant coach and Staffordshire U-16 player), Amritpal Singh, Jack Lewis, Ryan Singh, Dampreet Singh, Shoaib Malik, James Mackie, Prakesh Patel (team manager/coach), Dave Manning. Front Row: Ravi Kudhail, Mikesh Patel, Derek Underwood, Harjagdish Grewal, Wahab Malik (capt.), Jared Gill, Mrs Ann Barrington, Amanjot Jaswal, Ramonjot Jaswal.

The Wolverhampton U-13 Stafford Cup finalists in 2004. Left to right, back row: Joey Brew (the author), Andrew Gough, Sachin Rattu, Sham Patel, Dermot Jelfs, Georgia Elwiss, Charlotte Craddock. Front row: Andy Woollatt, Kuran Kumar, Jamil Khan. Andy Woollatt, Sham Patel, and Georgia Elwiss were all County U-13 players. Georgia is now an England U-21 international. Charlotte Craddock was the youngest member of the Great Britain Hockey Team at the Beijing Olympics in 2008.

Georgia Elwiss (back row, left) with the England U-21 side. Georgia had been playing for the Wolverhampton junior boys teams in each age group, and played senior men's cricket for Wolverhampton until moving to Meir Heath ladies team. She is currently the captain of Staffordshire. Elwiss is yet to make her full England debut, but was called into a provisional eighteen-woman squad for the T20 World Cup last year, so it will surely just be a matter of time.

ATHLETICS

Wolverhampton & Bilston Athletics Club, as the name suggests, was formed by the union of two athletics clubs after the town of Bilston was absorbed into the Borough of Wolverhampton in 1967. Before the First World War, there had been a Wolverhampton Cycling & Athletics Club, which used Molineux Grounds for training and for races, but when the football club expanded the stadium and did away with the running track, the town's athletes became homeless. A branch of Tipton Harriers used the ECC Sports ground, on Stafford Road, for a while in the early 1920s, and then in 1924, local athletes met in the Newhampton Hotel and formed Wolverhampton Athletics Club. There were other athletics clubs in the town, and they all mostly used the Sunbeam Athletics Club facilities, until the Sunbeam closed in 1935, after which they had a nomadic existence.

In 1943, Wolverhampton AC amalgamated with Penn Harriers, becoming Wolverhampton Harriers and using the Co-op's sports field on Compton Road, Tettenhall College playing fields, and then Marsh Lane playing fields. In 1956, athletics in the town made a huge leap forward when Aldersley Stadium was opened, as a home for the Harriers, and also Wolverhampton Wheelers Cycling Club, and other sports. A municipal sports stadium had first been mooted in 1937, but the war, and then the years of austerity afterwards, put the idea on the back burner. Land was earmarked on Autherley Farm, and in 1950, approval was finally given for a stadium to be the home of fifteen different sports. Then the fight for funding and construction took the next six years, but on 9 June 1956, the film star Jack Hawkins (who was in town making a film) finally opened one of the finest municipal stadiums in the country, with Wolverhampton Harriers one of its main tenants.

Bilston Athletics Club had been formed in 1951 and used a patch of grass in Hickman Park. Despite the small size of the club and its lack of facilities, Bilston AC managed to produce a number of nationally successful athletes. They made plans to create their own stadium on Great Bridge Road and raised money for its construction, but in 1967, the municipal boundary changes meant the town of Bilston was absorbed into its larger neighbour, and Bilston AC bowed to the inevitable and amalgamated with Wolverhampton Harriers to form Wolverhampton & Bilston Athletics Club.

The combined club was a powerful force, and when they joined the men's National Athletics League in 1970, they achieved three successive promotions to Division One, where they came third in their first season in 1972. In 1975, they were National Champions for the first time, going on to win the league eight times in a row from 1975 to 1982, doing the double in four of those years by also winning the National KO Cup. As National Champions, they went on to represent Great Britain in the European Clubs Competition, twice managing third place.

The women's Jubilee Cup was started in 1974, and W & B AC managed second place in this competition in 1975 and 1981. The British team that went to the European Championships in Berlin in 1971 included seven of the club's athletes: sprinters Jim Aukett, Don Halliday, Verona Bernard and Maureen Tranter, 800m runners Phil Lewis and Rosemary Stirling, and pole vaulter Mike Bull, who had joined the club from Northern Ireland.

The sheer dominance of Wolverhampton & Bilston during the 1970s and early 1980s was based on a number of fine coaches, like Charles Taylor with the sprinters and Ron Harris with the middle-distance runners, who attracted other runners to their 'stables' of athletes, but the club also enjoyed the proximity to RAF Cosford, which was at the time the only indoor athletics arena in Great Britain. Success bred more success, and individual athletes achieved a wealth of success in Commonwealth, European, World and Olympic Games.

The Club has declined somewhat in more recent years, most notably because the six-lane track at Aldersley is not permitted to host national meetings any more and cannot be expanded to eight lanes because of the cycle track surrounding it. Other reasons are the loss of some of the coaches, and with them their 'stable' of athletes, and the opening of indoor facilities in other parts of the country, but the club still has a membership of over 400, and still produces fine young athletes.

Above left: Wolverhampton Harriers runner, thirty-year-old Colin Kemball, with the magnificent trophy he won for coming first in the Windsor to Chiswick Polytechnic Marathon, run in conjunction with the AAA Marathon title in 1958. His winning time was 2 hours 22 minutes 27.4 seconds, in what was only his second marathon, being better known previously as a cross-country runner. He had competed in the AAA Marathon the year before, coming tenth in a time 8 minutes slower. As National Champion, he ran in the Empire Games Marathon, representing England.

Above right: A club dinner in the 1950s. Left to right: Ken Evans, a stalwart of the club for over sixty years, and for most of that time, the club secretary, Jack Sandbrook (Staffs AAA), Ray Edwards, Colin Kemball, receiving an award, and Reg Bradley (chairman).

Bilston-born Maureen Tranter, one of the finest British sprinters during the 1960s, starting a 220-yard race on a cinder track, probably at Smethwick. She joined Bilston Athletics Club and first came to national attention in 1962, as English Junior 150 yards Schools Champion. She was selected for the sprint-relay squad for the Tokyo Olympics in 1964, the first Olympian from Bilston AC. She broke the UK 440-yard Indoor Record at Cosford in 1965, followed by two indoor world records at 440 yards and 300 yards. She won Commonwealth silver in the 1966 sprint relay in Jamaica and was selected again for the Olympic sprint-relay squad in Mexico City. In 1968, she was a member of two world record-breaking squads at 4 x 110 yards and 4 x 200m. In the same year, she broke the individual UK and all-comers record for the 100 yards, at Birmingham, in a time of 10.6 seconds. She was selected in most of the squads for major championships up to her final Olympics in Munich in 1972, in the 4 x 400m. She started running as a veteran in 1994 and won a host of medals at major championships over the next ten years.

Peter Radford winning for Great Britain in a 200m race in a match against Italy. Radford was a Walsall-born Birchfield Harrier, but sneaks into this book because he broke the World 200m Record at Aldersley Stadium, the only world record broken there. On 28 May 1960, he set a new world record of 20.5 seconds for the 220 yards, at Aldersley, which was also recognised as a 200m record. He won gold at the Commonwealth Games in both 1958 and 1962 in the 110-yard relay, and in the European Championships, he won bronze in the 1958 100m and silver in the 100m relay. In the 1960 Olympics, he won bronze in both the 100m and the 4 x 100m relay, but lost out in his favourite, 200m, coming fourth in his semi-final, the victim of poor seeding. Radford's other world record was in the Great Britain squad in 1963, running the now-almost-forgotten 110-yard relay. His appearances at Aldersley drew crowds of up to 10,000 people to the stadium.

Dave Guest, Wolverhampton & Bilston's club captain, holding aloft the National League Division One trophy in 1975. The club won the National League eight times in a row from 1975 to 1982, going on to represent Great Britain each following year in the European Clubs Cup, with a best finish of third. Dave Guest usually ran the 800m, but occasionally ran 1,500m or, if pressed, the 5,000m. He also ran the 800m leg when the club broke the national indoor medley relay record at Cosford (100m, 200m, 400m, 800m). He came within one place of an international vest one year, when coming fourth in the AAA indoor 800m final at Cosford.

The Wolverhampton & Bilston Athletics Club team after winning the men's National KO Cup at Crystal Palace in 1976. They also won this trophy in 1977, 1979, and 1980, thereby achieving the League/Cup double, more times than any football team. During this period, the club were easily the best athletics club in the country. Their decline began when they could no longer use their home Aldersley Stadium track to host National League meetings because it only had six lanes and could not be expanded because of the surrounding cycle track.

Charles Taylor, the club's sprinting coach, with the WBAC team, which won the AAA's indoor 4 x 100m relay title at Cosford in March 1968. Left to right: Gwynne Griffiths, Alan Jones, Taylor (then also club chairman), Ralph Banthorpe, Roger Walters. All these four sprinters won international vests. Ralph Banthorpe was a semi-finalist in the 200m at the Mexico Olympics in 1968.

Four well-known members of Wolverhampton & Bilston. Left to right: Phil Lewis (800m runner in his GB tracksuit) Ron Harris (the club's middle-distance coach), Rosemary Stirling (in her GB tracksuit) and Rob Stirling (Rosemary's brother and also an 800m runner). Rosemary Stirling ran 38 times for Great Britain, but won gold in the 1970 Commonwealth Games in Edinburgh in the 800m, running for Scotland. She was born in New Zealand but came to live in Claregate. She also won gold in the 1969 European Championships and the 1970 European Cup, (in the 4 x 400m relay team), came third in the European indoor 800m and the 1971 European Championship, and reached the Olympic 800m final in 1972 coming seventh in a British National Record time of 2.01.1. She was also part of the British team which twice broke the world record for the 4 x 800m in 1970. In an era when women were not allowed to compete at distances greater than 800m, all runners at this distance faced fierce competition. She married the marathon runner Trevor Wright and now lives in New Zealand.

Phil Lewis winning the AAA's junior 880-yard title at Aldersley Stadium, just beating J. V. James of Wales, who later also joined Wolverhampton & Bilston. In 1971, Lewis won the national indoors 800m title.

Wolverhampton-born Verona Elder, who was to set a record for appearances in the Great Britain team and appeared in three Olympics. The 400m was her event, and she was AAA's champion in 1976 and 1977, second in 1978 and 1979, and third in 1980. She twice won silver in the Commonwealth individual 400m, in 1974 as Verona Bernard in a time of 51.94 seconds, and in 1978, with her married name of Verona Elder, in a whole second slower, but that year won gold in the 4 x 400m. She had a run of success in the European Indoor Championships, winning gold in the 400m three times, in 1973, 1975 and 1979, silver in 1977, and bronze in 1981.

Tessa Sanderson, one of Wolverhampton & Bilston's finest athletes, who won the Olympic gold medal for the javelin in 1984 in Los Angeles, as well as European silver in 1978 and Commonwealth golds in 1978, 1986 and 1990. She was a fine all-round athlete who could have been a world-class Heptathlete if she had concentrated on that event. She had started out as a multi-event athlete, and came fifth in the national women's pentathlete championship when only seventeen, in 1973. Her real breakthrough in the javelin was later that year, when she surprisingly won the Commonwealth Games Trials with a throw of 51.34m. She came fifth in the Commonwealth Games in New Zealand the following January, and the way was clear for continued progression towards becoming a top-class expert in the javelin. At her first Olympics in Montreal, she finished tenth but broke the UK National Record three times. In fact, she eventually broke the record ten times, with a personal best of 73.58m. She was ranked as UK No. 1 in the javelin ten times, and No. 2 seven times. She was the top Heptathlete in 1981, and was ranked in the top six for both the 100m and the 400m hurdles.

One of the finest British sprinters of her era, Birmingham-born Sonia Lannaman. She won Olympic bronze in the 4 x 100m in 1980, and European silver in the same event in 1978. In the Commonwealth Games, she won sprint relay silver in 1974 and gold in 1982, but her finest Championships was undoubtedly 1978, when she won gold in the individual 100m, silver in the 200m, and gold in the sprint relay.

Kathy Cook, a Wolverhampton Sporting Hero by marriage, here winning a bronze medal in the 1984 Olympics in Los Angeles in the 400m, where she won another bronze in the 4 x 100m relay. As Kathy Smallwood, she became one of Great Britain's greatest ever sprinters at Reading Athletic Club and still holds the British National Records for 200m, 300m, 400m, and 4 x 100m. In addition, she also held the British record for 100m from 1981 to 2008.

She qualifies for inclusion in this book because she married Wolverhampton & Bilston 800m runner Garry Cook. Garry Cook won an Olympic silver medal in the 4 x 400m relay in the 1984 Olympics in LA having won bronze in the previous year's World Championships in the same event. He broke the world record in the rarely run 4 x 800m in 1982 with his team-mates Peter Elliot, Sebastian Coe and Steve Cram, three names which help suggest why he did not win more individual medals, just as Kathy might have won more if she had not been competing against East European athletes who have since been proven to have used drugs.

Kathy, who became a member of W & B AC after marrying Garry, won a total of fifteen medals at major championships. Apart from her two in LA, she also won a bronze in the 1980 Moscow Olympics in the 4 x 100, two silvers in the 1983 World Championships in the 200m and the 4 x 100m, three silvers in the Europeans, two in the 4 x 100 in 1978 and 1982, and in 1982, the 200m. In three Commonwealth Games, she twice won gold in the 4 x 100, three times silver, twice in the 200m and once in the 4 x 400m, and bronze in the 1986 400m. After 1986, she retired from athletics to start a family, and both she and Garry are now teachers in Walsall.

Wolverhampton & Bilston's junior team at Swansea in 1985 after finishing fourth in the Dunlop Young Athletics League. Dave Guest, now a coach for the club, is on the left, still a club stalwart after forty years. Part of the reason for the decline of the club over the last couple of decades was the loss of one or two important coaches, and their groups of athletes. Talented athletes naturally gravitate to coaches with an existing 'stable' of successful athletes. Success naturally fosters further success.

Although born in West Bromwich and a Birchfield Harrier, Denise Lewis has always been regarded as one of Wolverhampton's own, as she was brought up in the town. One of the finest all-round athletes of her generation, she won Olympic gold in the year 2000 in Sydney, after achieving bronze in 1996. She won World Championship silver in 1997 and 1999, European gold in 1998, and Commonwealth golds in 1994 and 1998. She had been recognised as an all-round athlete at an early age, at Birchfield. By 1991, still only nineteen, she was already ranked in the UK top three, and progressed steadily to her first Commonwealth Gold medal, in Canada, in 1994.

Denise Lewis hurdling her way to World Championship silver in Athens in 1997. She was a fine 100m hurdler in her own right and ranked as high as second in Great Britain in the individual long jump.

JUDO

Arguably, Wolverhampton Judo Club is the most successful sporting club in the city. In its relatively short history of just over forty years, it has been a production line of champions, often dominating the British men's judo team. The current club was born in 1966, formed by two members of the previous Wolverhampton Judo Club, which was based in Temple Street, but which ran into financial difficulties. Mac Abbotts and Dave Brooks were the prime movers in creating a new organisation based at Heath Town Baths, with a philosophy of members competing in as many competitions as possible.

In 1974, Mac Abbotts was employed by Wolverhampton Borough Council as judo instructor in local schools, and this enabled him to identify and recruit young talent, which began to dominate national junior competitions, juniors who became some of the major names in British senior judo, with the seven-man Great Britain World and Olympic teams often made up of a majority of Wolverhampton players, who were multiple National Champions: e.g., Kerrith Brown ten times, Dennis Stewart five times, Densign White nine times, Elvis Gordon six times, Fitzroy Davis twice, Owen Pinnock once, and John Swatman twice.

Craig Fallon became World 60kg Champion in Cairo in 2005. Only the third British fighter to win the world title, he followed this up by winning the European gold the following year. He had taken silver in both events previously. Ipswich-born Fallon began with the Wolverhampton Judo Club but, while still a teenager, moved to the National Judo Academy in Buckinghamshire to further his career. Fallon fought for Great Britain in the Athens Olympics, and the Beijing Olympics, just losing the fight for the bronze medal.

Wolverhampton had shown the way and became a virtual national judo academy, but nowadays promising young judo players are whisked away to the new National Performance Institute at Dartford, overseen by the Chairman of the British Judo Association, Densign White. The latest has been Gemma Howell, who started at Wolverhampton, and is now an exciting prospect for the 2012 Olympics.

The Jack Law Memorial Trophy Tournament players in January 1976. Left to right, back row: Corbett Scarlett (silver), Dave Thompson (gold), Simon Edmonds (gold), Robert Prosser (silver), Kevin Blower (gold), Mark Swatman (silver). Front row: John Swatman (silver), Kerrith Brown (silver), John Ward (silver), Martin Downes (silver), Tom Brindle (silver). Kerrith Brown and John Swatman became part of the 1984 British Olympic Judo Team in Los Angeles, with Kerrith winning a bronze medal, and at Seoul four years later.

Above: The Midland Area Judo Team who were National Champions ten out of eleven years. Their one loss was in 1984, when four of the usual team (all from Wolverhampton) were away training for the Olympics. Left to right: Fitzroy Davis, Owen Pinnock, Elvis Gordon, Densign White, Dale Webb (the only player not from Wolverhampton), Michael Chamberlain, and Richard West in front.

Right: Bronze medallists at the 1987 World Championships at Essen, Densign White (u86kg on the left) and Kerrith Brown (u71kg). Densign White was National Champion nine times, and represented Great Britain three times at the Olympics from Los Angeles onwards. He later became Chairman of the British Judo Association. Kerrith Brown won bronze for Great Britain at the 1984 Olympics and was National Champion at his weight ten times.

Wolverhampton Judo Club team for the second rounds of the European Club Championship versus TSV München-Großhadern, which took place at Compton Park, and resulted in a 5 v 1 win for Wolves. Left to right, back row: Elvis Gordon, Fitzroy Davis, Densign White, Dennis Stewart. Front row: Kerrith Brown, John Swatman, Owen Pinnock, Kenneth Dodd. The team went on to beat Racing Club of France in the semi-final, and again won 5 v 1, to face USO Orleans in the final.

The Wolverhampton Judo Club team, runners-up in the 1986 European Team Championship at a civic reception. They had lost the first leg 1 v 2, won the second leg 3 v 2, but lost a three-fight play-off 1 v 2. Left to right, back row: Elvis Gordon, Dennis Stewart, Densign White, Mayor Bishen Dass, John Bird (MEP), Kerrith Brown, Kenneth Dodd, Fitzroy Davis, the Mayoress, Dave Brooks (coach). Front row: John Swatman, Owen Pinnock, Mac Abbotts (coach).

Elvis Gordon, the first Englishman to win a judo gold medal on Japanese soil, in the Matsutaro-Shoriki Cup, Elvis represented Great Britain at three Olympics, his first being Los Angeles in 1984, when he was twenty-six, followed by Seoul and Barcelona. He won a silver medal in the 1987 World Championships, a gold and two bronzes at European Championships, and two gold medals at Commonwealth Games.

The 1988 Great Britain Judo Team in Seoul. Left to right, back row: Elvis Gordon (Wolverhampton), Dennis Stewart (Wolverhampton – bronze medallist), Arthur Mapp (team manager). Middle row: Mac Abbotts (coach – Wolverhampton), Neal Adams. Front row: Mark Adshead, Ken Kingsbury (team doctor), Neal Eckersley, Kerrith Brown (Wolverhampton). Densign White (Wolverhampton) is not in the picture for some reason.

On the left is Mac Abbotts (Wolverhampton Judo Club founder and coach) fighting in the 1981 Black Country Olympics, which he won. Though something of a veteran at the time, he felt he had better win, considering the achievements of his protégés.

Gemma Howell, who became bronze medal winner at both the World and European Junior Championships in her under 57kg division. Nurtured at Wolverhampton, she was soon whisked away to be under Densign White's wing at the National Institute at Dartford, with her family moving down there to give her every chance of prospering in the 2012 Olympics.

CYCLING

Cycle manufacture was a major business in Wolverhampton in the nineteenth century, and cycle racing was a sport which attracted huge interest. The major cycle racing track was in the grounds of Molineux House, where the Wolves stadium is now situated, and crowds of up to 30,000 people came to see the races, bringing in racing cyclists from all over the country. There were as many as thirty cycle manufacturers in the town, ranging from the 'Rolls-Royce' of bicycles made by Sunbeam to small back-street operations. One of the biggest was Viking, which was founded in 1908, and later moved to Princess Alley. In 1948, they formed a successful racing team, lead by Bob Thom, one of the greatest racing cyclists of his day, and a member of the Wolverhampton Wheelers cycling club from 1935. Many cycling clubs sprang up across the town, but the main one was the Wheelers.

Wolverhampton Wheelers Cycling Club has been one of the most established and most successful sporting clubs in Wolverhampton since being founded in 1891. The club has been based at Aldersley Leisure Village since 1956 and has produced many cyclists that have gone on to compete in international age group and senior competitions for Great Britain. Most probably, its most successful protégé is Hugh Porter, MBE, who won four world individual pursuit titles between 1968 and 1973, along with several national championships, as well as being an Olympian in 1964. A more recent cyclist to come out of the 'Wheelers' is Andy Tennant, who won the Individual Pursuit title at the World Junior Championships in 2005 and the Team Pursuit title at the European U23 Championships in 2006. In 2009, in Manchester, he was a member of the four-man pursuit team that won the Team World Cup in the second-fastest time ever. Another club member, Percy Stallard, was one of the key movers in forming the British League of Racing Cyclists, which sought and eventually succeeded in overthrowing the law that disallowed road racing in Britain.

Left: Norman Haselock, one of the leading lights in the formation of the British League of Racing Cyclists, shown near the finish of the 1937 Speedwell 100 held at Tewkesbury. The National Cyclists Union would only organise individual time trials such as this, for fear of falling foul of the police if they were to approve the sort of mass road races (like the Tour of France), which were accepted in the rest of the World. Haselock and Percy Stallard were instrumental in changing that.

Below left: Norman Haselock competing in the Penn Common Cyclo-Cross in 1948. It was normal for cyclists in those days to retain their fitness through the winter months by competing in cyclo-cross events, though it's hard to see a great deal of similarity between the sports, apart from the involvement of the bike.

Bob Thom coming sixth in the first London to Holyhead race in 1951. He had joined Wolverhampton Wheelers in 1935 aged just seventeen and won the first handicap prize in his first race. Percy Stallard took an interest in the young rider, helping him become very successful, winning the Midland Area Championship aged twenty-one, and in 1938 coming sixth in the National Championships. The war robbed him of what would probably have been his best years, and he served in the RAF in Rhodesia. He was twenty-nine when he was demobbed, and rejoined the Wheelers, but after a year, became a professional, joining Percy Stallard's British League of Racing Cyclists, and his first win was the 100km Circuit of Dudley. When Viking Cycles formed a racing team in 1948, Thom was made Rider/Manager. He also became British Team Manager.

Opposite, below right: Percy Stallard, one of the most famous names in British cycle racing, shown here at Brooklands in 1934. Stallard was born at his father's cycle shop in Broad Street in 1909. He joined the Wolverhampton Wheelers in 1927 and by 1933 was in the British team in the road racing World Championships, coming eleventh, the first Briton home, and coming seventh the following year. Road racing on the Continent was a massed start event, but in Britain was restricted to individual time trials. Stallard campaigned for massed start events and organised the first from Llangollen to Wolverhampton in 1942, despite being banned by the National Cycling Union, the governing body. Stallard formed the British League of Racing Cyclists and the two rival bodies fought a bitter war until their eventual merger in 1959. Throughout this period, Stallard organised and rode in massed road races, and rode in his last race when he was fifty-six. He was an energetic and enlightened man who brought the Tour de France type of race to this country and was one of the finest British cyclists of his day, but he was hard to get along with and even fell out with both the BLRC and the League of Veteran Racing Cyclists, which he also formed.

Viking Cycles' 1951 Team. From the left: B. Whitmore, Bob Thom, F. Nicholls, J. Welch, T. Jones. This was the year Bob retired from competitive racing, but remained team manager. He also worked as Viking's sales manager and became British Team Manager, taking them to many team victories, including the Tour of Holland and the Tour of Sweden. Viking Cycles went from strength to strength and, by 1963, had an annual production of 20,000 cycles, but then they began to struggle and, in 1967, were sold to Americans, who moved the business to California, Bob Thom going with them for a couple of years.

Opposite above: At full speed at an indoor velodrome, Hugh Porter, the most famous of all the town's racing cyclists, born in Wolverhampton in 1940, and a pupil of St Peter's Collegiate School. His father, Joe, was a cyclist, and Hugh became a member of the Wheelers when he was sixteen, coming third in his first race. He soon began winning road races as a senior and won a gold medal as part of the Wheelers Pursuit Team at the National Championships in 1959. In the early 1960s, he raced for Great Britain on the road, and following a win in the Midland Individual Pursuit began developing his track-racing expertise. In 1963, he won the first of three successive national titles and reached the semi-final stage of the World Championships. The 1964 Olympics in Tokyo were a disappointment: he was eliminated at the quarter final stage. He continued to win road races and in 1967 turned professional. He won his first professional 5,000m pursuit title in 1968, having come second the year before. In 1969, he won silver again and, in 1970, won gold on home territory at Leicester. In 1971, he won bronze, but in the following two years, he won gold yet again, to complete a total of four world titles.

Below: Hugh with his MBE at Buckingham Palace, with his mother, and on the right his wife, the Olympic gold medal-winning swimmer, Anita Lonsbrough, who he met at Tokyo and married in 1965. Another honour bestowed upon him was the naming of the approach road to Aldersley Stadium, Hugh Porter Way, a fitting reminder to all the cyclists making their way to the Wheelers' home track of his cycling exploits, though for many years he has been usually better known as the voice of BBC cycling commentaries.

Left: Andy Tennant, another Wolverhampton-born cyclist who is quickly making a name for himself on the world stage. In 2005, he was sponsored by Fred Williams Cycles, and he became World Junior Individual Pursuit Champion in Austria, taking a silver in the team pursuit. In 2009, he was part of the British four-man pursuit team who won the World Cup title in 3 minutes 54.395 seconds, only bettered by the Beijing winning team.

Below: Andy Tennant, on the left, riding in the Tour of Britain for Team Halfords in 2006. They are in the area of Sheffield, and leading at this point is Tom Boonen, the Belgian 2005 World Road Race Champion. Next to Andy is Mark Cavendish, who won four stages on the 2008 Tour de France, then a British record, and surpassed it with six wins the following year.

SPEEDWAY

The 'other' team called Wolves in Wolverhampton is the Speedway team, who race at Monmore Green Stadium. Speedway was first promoted at Monmore Green in 1928 just after speedway was first introduced to Great Britain, but only lasted until 1930. A new team was formed twenty years later as the Wolverhampton Wasps, riding in the National League Division Three in 1951. The following year, the team merged with Cradley Heath, and though the resulting team rode at Monmore Green, they took the Heathens' Division Two place. They faired badly and folded in 1954. The Wolves reappeared in 1961, riding in the Midland League Championship, winning it in 1962, and also in the Provincial League, becoming champions of that in 1963.

Apart from a couple of seasons, the Wolves have ridden consistently in the top flight of British Speedway, becoming British League Champions in 1991, Premier League winners in 1996, and Elite League Champions in 2002, and for the second time in 2009.

Two World Speedway Champions have raced for Wolves. The Dane, Ole Olsen, won the world title in 1971 and 1975 while at Wolves, and for a third time in 1978 after he had left Wolves. The American, Sam Ermolenko, became World Champion while at Wolves in 1993. Two riders have become World Under-21 Champions while at Wolves, Mikael Karlsson in 1994 and Jesper B. Jensen in 1991 and 1994.

The 1963 Wolverhampton Wolves, winners of the Provincial League Championship in that year. The team of this era, promoted by Bill Bridgett, including such riders as Tommy Sweetman (captain), Pete Jarman, Colin McKee, Cyril Francis, Jim Airey, Harry Edwards and James Bond (whose number was not 007).

Ole Olsen, the Dane who rode for the Wolves from 1970 to 1975, was World Champion in 1971 and 1975 (and for a third time, after leaving Wolves, in 1978). His fame transcended the sport, and his name was often chanted at the Molineux during the early 1970s. As well as his two world titles, while at Wolves, he was also British League Riders Champion in 1972. He also won this championship after leaving Wolves for the Coventry Bees, in 1976, 1977 and 1978.

Ole Olsen riding during his second World Championship-winning performance, in 1975, wearing the Danish flag. At the time, he was the biggest sports star in Denmark and helped popularise the sport there. He built his own track at Vajens. After leaving Wolves, he rode for the Coventry Bees.

Right: The Californian, Sam Ermolenko, who rode for Wolves from 1986 to 1995, and captained them to the British League title in 1991. After a year at Sheffield Tigers and one at Belle Vue Aces, he came back to Wolves in 1998, but then had a year with Hull Vikings, a year back with Wolves in 2001, and another year at the Aces, before returning to Wolves for his final stint 2003-04.

Below: Sam Ermolenko in action at Monmore Green. He became World Champion in 1993 at Pockling, Germany, and was also British League Rider's Champion in 1991 and 1994 (and 1996 while at the Tigers). He had been US Champion in 1993 and 1994. After retiring from riding, he managed Reading in 2006, and became Sky's Speedway commentator.

Upper: 'Rocket' Ronnie Correy, another American who starred at Wolves in two stints from 1987 to 1993 and 1996 to 1997, having fun with the Wolves' mascot, Wolfman. He helped them to the British League title in 1991 and the British League title in 1996. He became World Pairs Champion in 1992, and was a member of the US team that won the World Team Cup in the same year. In 1996, Wolves achieved a unique League and Cup double when they won the Speedway Star Knockout Cup. Ronnie retired in 2000 due to injury, though he did have two short comebacks with Belle Vue and Edinburgh.

Lower: Wolverhampton Wolves 2009 Elite League winners, a multi-national team. Back row: Chris Kerr (California, USA), Tyron Proctor (Australia), Nicolai Klindt (Denmark), Tai Woffinden (Scunthorpe, Lincs), Adam Skornicki (Poland). Front row: holding the Elite League Cup, Freddie Lindgren (Sweden), Peter Karlsson, (captain, Sweden). Freddie Lindren was voted the Elite League's top rider of 2009 by the Speedway Rider's Association, and was the highest average points scorer for the season. Peter Karlsson is a Wolves legend, riding for them in most seasons since 1990.

AIR RACING

Air racing is not one of the sports anyone would immediately associate with Wolverhampton, and yet the town has had an involvement with the sport from the very earliest days, and for many years staged one of the country's premier air races, the Goodyear Trophy. Local pilots have also featured heavily in what is admittedly a minority sport, but one which, on occasions, has drawn huge crowds.

The first ever all-British Flying Meeting (and only the third in all) was held at Dunstall Park in June 1910 and featured a number of aerial competitions, though none were races in the accepted sense. None of the aircraft competing and none of the pilots were Wolverhampton-born, but this state of affairs was soon to change. In 1912, the Sunbeam Motor Car Company, already heavily committed to motor racing at Brooklands and elsewhere, decided to enter the world of aviation. Their mercurial chief designer Louis Coatalen, designed a 150-hp V8 aero-engine, and to test it, the company purchased a Farman biplane and engaged a young pilot named Jack Alcock, whose name will forever be associated with that of Arthur Whitten Brown, since together they became the first men to fly the Atlantic non-stop, in 1919.

The Farman was based at Brooklands, where it was 'in the shop window' and could be supported by Sunbeam's racing car team. It was entered in virtually every major air race pre-war.

Air racing resumed after the First World War, without a great deal of local involvement. The premier air race in Great Britain has always been the King's Cup, a handicap event which has been organised annually since 1922 at various venues. In 1950, it was held at Wolverhampton Airport, Pendeford, with three laps over a 100-km course, with turning points at Abbots Bromley, Stoke Airport, and Newport. It was won by Edward Day flying a Miles Hawk Trainer, with the Hawker Hurricane G-AMAU *The Last of the Many* just second, in the colours of Princess Margaret. It was being flown by one Group Captain Peter Townsend.

Ron Paine, Surrey-born, but with long connections with Wolverhampton, came second in the King's Cup no fewer than five times in his Miles Hawk Speed Six. He had become chief engineer with Air Schools at Wolverhampton Airport during the war, and was to remain at Pendeford well into the 1950s. In 1963, the King's Cup was won by a local man, Paul Bannister, flying his Pendeford-based little Tipsy Nipper, G-APYB. He had only learned to fly, at Wolverhampton, in 1958, and after winning the King's Cup at his second attempt, he was to reflect that, after two years of air racing, he still had not overtaken anyone! This was, of course, because his little 45-hp Nipper, under the handicap system, was always the first starter.

The Goodyear Trophy Race was another handicap air race, sponsored by Goodyear Tyres and run annually. It took place at Wolverhampton Airport, until that closed, and then moved the short distance to Halfpenny Green.

A young Jack Alcock standing in front of his Sunbeam-powered Farman biplane. This Manchester lad had made his name as a pilot and engineer at Brooklands and was the ideal recruit to test Sunbeam's new 150-hp V8 aero-engine in the French Farman biplane bought to test it. Alcock piloted the aircraft in the 1913 Aerial Derby around London on 6 June, but dropped out, probably because of the bad weather. On 20 June, he raced in the London-Manchester-London two-day air race, and came third: the first time a British-powered aircraft had even finished a long-distance air race. Alcock served in the Royal Naval Air Service during the war, mostly in the Balkans, where he had the distinction of building his 'own' aircraft, mostly out of spare parts. After the war, he returned to life as a test pilot, and with Arthur Whitten Brown as navigator, on 14 June 1919, became the first to fly the Atlantic non-stop. He died on 18 December while flying a Vickers Viking aircraft, to the Paris Air Show, crashing in bad weather in Normandy, aged only twenty-seven.

Ron Paine, on the right, with Eric Holden, Wolverhampton Airport Manager. Paine was one of a group of air racers who earned the nickname 'The Throttlebenders' in the 1950s. He raced his pre-war specially built air racer, the Miles Hawk Speed Six, shown below, in handicap air races, and was usually scratch aircraft, i.e., fastest and therefore last away, having to overtake everything else in order to win. He never managed to win the King's Cup, coming second a record five times, in each case setting the fastest time. He had started out as an aircraft engineer at Brooklands in 1932, and learned to fly in the late 1930s. He joined Derby Aviation, who operated the RAF's flying training school at Wolverhampton during the war, and ran the airport after the war. Six Miles Gemini aircraft were assembled by the company, from parts obtained from the demise of Miles Aircraft, and one of these was modified and tested by Paine for the legless wartime fighter ace, Douglas Bader, who worked for Shell. Paine bought the Hawk Speed Six from the remains of Miles Aircraft at the same time, and owned it for the next seventeen years.

A Wolverhampton-based aircraft which did win the King's Cup was this little Tipsy Nipper, G-APYB, powered by a Volkswagen-based engine. Flown by local man Paul Bannister, it came first at Baginton, Coventry, in 1963 at 102.5 mph.

The LeVier Cosmic Wind, G-ARUL Ballerina, being started by Bill Innes just before the 1966 Goodyear Air Trophy Race at Halfpenny Green. This American aircraft was one of three specially built in 1947-48 by Lockheed pilots and engineers for racing in the American Goodyear Trophy, and was capable of 188 mph on only 85 hp. Just after this picture was taken, Innes took off at the start of the race, stalled while rounding the first turn and crashed. Innes survived, but the Cosmic Wind was wrecked. Paul Bannister bought the remains and spent much of the 1970s rebuilding it, though he subsequently sold it.

MOTOR RACING

Although Wolverhampton currently has little connection with the world of motor racing, this was not always the case. When the town rivalled Coventry as the motor-manufacturing capital of the country, with major names like Star, Sunbeam, Clyno, Guy, and AJS, the Frenchman Louis Herve Coatalen brought much motor-racing success to the town. After eight years as chief engineer at Humber in Coventry, Coatalen was recruited in the same role by the Sunbeam Motor Car Company of Wolverhampton. He believed that racing improves the breed and designed a series of racing cars, which achieved great success, including winning the 1912 Coupe de l'Auto in France, the 1914 Isle of Man TT, and breaking eight closed circuit world records at Brooklands in a car named Toodles V. The premier motor race in the world was the French Grand Prix, and it was his great ambition to win it. After several creditable attempts, a Sunbeam finally became the first British racing car to win this race in 1923, driven by Henry Segrave.

Coatalen then turned his attention to the World Land Speed Record, and Sunbeam cars broke this record five times. On 17 May 1922, Kenelm Lee Guinness achieved 133.7 mph in the 350-hp Sunbeam, built round a special V12 Sunbeam Manitou aero-engine. This was the last time the World Speed Record was set on a closed circuit, at Brooklands. After this car was extensively streamlined, with the help of the Boulton & Paul wind tunnel in Norwich, Malcolm Campbell twice used it to break the record again, this time over the measured mile on Pendine Sands, achieving 146.15 mph on 25 September 1924 and 150.86 mph on 21 July 1925 (the first car over 150 mph). On 21 March 1926, Henry Segrave broke the record, in a 4-litre Sunbeam Tiger, on Southport Sands, and then became the first man over 200 mph in the 1,000-hp Sunbeam, powered by two 400+hp Matabele aero-engines, achieving 203.79 mph on Daytona Beach.

Though Coatalen made one more attempt to break the Land Speed Record with the beautiful Silver Bullet, in 1930, the parent company was in severe financial difficulty and, after its failure, was forced to pull out of motor sport. Louis Coatalen returned to France soon afterwards, and the Sunbeam Motor Car Co. was bought out by the Rootes Brothers in 1935 and closed down.

Left: The most unlikely of all Wolverhampton's sporting heroes was the Frenchman Louis Coatalen, the chief engineer of the Sunbeam Motor Car Company from 1909 almost until its demise in 1935. He designed many successful racing cars, but his greatest achievements were designing the first British car to win the French Grand Prix in 1923, and three different world speed record-breaking cars, including the first car to exceed 150 mph and the first to exceed 200 mph, bringing fame to Sunbeam and to the town.

Below: The Sunbeam racing car Toodles V at Brooklands in 1913. Powered by a 200-hp V12 engine, the car broke eight world endurance records (over different distances) in an hour and a half. The engine was the prototype for the Sunbeam Mohawk aero-engine, the most powerful British engine available in the first years of the Great War.

The 350-hp Sunbeam on Pendine Sands, where it twice broke the World Land Speed Record, in 1924 and 1925, becoming the first car to exceed 150 mph. It had already held the record, set at Brooklands: the last time it was set over a closed circuit, rather than two straight-line runs, in opposite directions. It had been raced at Brooklands by the famous test pilot Harry Hawker who said of Coatalen's team, 'The Sunbeam people do the whole thing properly.'

Malcolm Campbell seated in the 350-hp Sunbeam, which was powered by a modified V12 Sunbeam Manitou aero-engine, and the streamlined nose and tail were tested in the Boulton & Paul wind tunnel in Norwich. The car is currently displayed in the National Motor Museum at Beaulieu. The car was unofficially named Bluebird, the first of Campbell's cars to carry that name.

Henry Segrave in the Sunbeam Tiger racing car on Southport Sands where he broke the World Land Speed Record, just taking it from Malcom Campbell's 350-hp Sunbeam in 1926 with a speed of 152.3 mph. At a clear rebuff to his great rival Campbell, he nicknamed the car Ladybird.

The Sunbeam Experimental Shop at the Moorfield Works in the early 1920s, with Grand Prix racing cars being prepared. This building still exists, now offices, though the large lift that carried the cars to the upper floors is still in place. It is a sad testament to the decline of a great company that the adjacent building is now used to store Mercedes-Benz cars by the local dealership. Hundreds of cars made by Sunbeam's main German rival now pass within a few feet of the building where world war aero-engines and fine racing cars were developed.

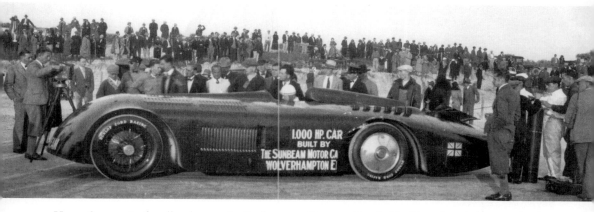

Henry Segrave in the all-red 1,000-hp Sunbeam on Daytona Beach, Florida, where it became the first car in the world to exceed 200 mph on 29 March 1927. The specially made car, powered by two V12 Sunbeam Matabele aero-engines was nicknamed 'The Slug'. It had broken the record by the widest margin ever, eclipsing a time set by Malcolm Campbell in his second Bluebird, a Napier-powered car.

Sunbeam's last attempt at the Land Speed Record was undertaken by this car, named Silver Bullet, in March 1930. Driven at Daytona Beach by Kaye Don, and powered by two specially made V12 engines, each said, by Louis Coatalen, to give 1,000 hp, the car suffered severe technical difficulties, and only ever managed 186 mph, though it did break the American 5-km record. With Sunbeam in financial difficulties, it was their last hurrah in motor sport.

Richard Attwood is a Wolverhampton-born sports car and Formula 1 racing driver. In Formula 1, he drove for BRM, Lotus, and Cooper variously, in the years 1964 to 1969, and garnered a total of eleven World Championship points, with a second at Monaco behind Graham Hill being his best result. His finest racing achievement was winning the Le Mans 24-hour race in a Porsche 917 with co-driver Hans Hermann, in 1970, as shown below. He retired from racing after the 1984 Le Mans race, when his Aston Martin failed to finish.

MOTORCYCLE RACING

It's now hard to imagine Wolverhampton as being one of the powerhouses of motorcycle racing, but in the 1920s, it was Wolverhampton motorcycles that usually led the way in the prestigious Isle of Man TT races and elsewhere. As well as three major names in motorcycle manufacture, Sunbeam, AJS and Clyno, the town also boasted many other marques, including Star, Diamond, Orbit, HRD, and Wearwell's Wolf and Wulfruna brands. From 1914 onwards, the workers, in the Blakenhall area of the town in particular, waited impatiently every year to hear how 'their' bikes had fared on the Isle of Man.

To begin with, it was usually AJS triumphant in the Junior TT (Mostly for 350 cc bikes) and Sunbeam in the Senior TT (for up to 500 cc bikes). In 1914, AJS were first and second in the Junior, and Sunbeam second in the Senior. When motorcycle racing resumed in 1920, it was a double for the town, AJS first in the Junior TT, Sunbeam first and third in the Senior. The following year was even more triumphant, with AJS taking the first four places in the Junior TT, and also winning the Senior, where H. R. Davies rode his Junior bike to victory after coming second in the Junior race. 1922 was another double victory, AJS first and second in the Junior, Sunbeam first, sixth and eighth in the Senior.

For the next three years, Sunbeam struggled to keep pace, and AJS did not manage any wins, though they did usually manage second or third in one or both races, but by now, Wolverhampton had a third manufacturer competing. H. R. Davies had started his own company using his initials as the name and was gloriously triumphant in his first TT meeting as a manufacturer. In 1925, he came second on his HRD in the Junior TT behind a Rex-Acme, beating Jimmy Simpson's AJS into third place, and won the Senior TT, beating Frank Longman's AJS into second place.

The following year, Wolverhampton had four motorcycle manufacturers sending teams to the island, as Diamond entered the Lightweight TT (for 175 cc bikes), and Sid Gleave came seventh on his. In the Junior TT, AJS came second, seventh and eighth, but in the Senior TT, seven Wolverhampton bikes came in the top ten. AJS were third and sixth, HRD were fifth, eighth and ninth, and Sunbeam were seventh, and tenth.

In their short three-year existence, HRD were to have one more win on the island, in the 1927 Junior TT. Sunbeam were to have two, in the 1928 Senior, when an AJS was second, and the 1929 Senior, with another Sunbeam second. Though they were usually to be found in the top ten of both races from 1927 to 1930, AJS managed no more wins, except in a rare outing in the 1930 Lightweight TT, when they came first and fifth.

In the first years of the 1930s, both teams struggled, never featuring in the top five in any race, and by the middle of the decade, both manufacturing concerns had been sold, for their brand names and goodwill, and the Wolverhampton factories were closed down.

The Sunbeam Team for the 1914 Isle of Man Senior TT race. From the left: Tommy de la Hay (who would win the Senior TT in 1920 on his Sunbeam), Vernon Busby, Howard Davies, and Charlie Noakes. Sunbeam won the Team Prize with Davies coming second individually. Davies, normally known as H. R. Davies, was the most notable of the four. He started with AJS in Retreat Street and then joined Sunbeam via a spell at Clyno. He became a pilot during the First World War, and afterwards rejoined AJS, becoming their competitions manager, turning them into a force to be reckoned with. In the 1921 TT Races, AJS machines filled the first four places in the Junior TT, with Davies coming second, despite a puncture, and then he won the Senior TT. After a few poor years with AJS, Davies formed his own motorcycle company, HRD Motors, also in Wolverhampton, and in 1926, he won the Senior TT and came second in the Junior TT.

H. F. Harris with his 1922 Junior TT AJS motorcycle, behind one of the grandstands. He did not manage to finish the race that year, but the AJS team once again took the Team Prize. The following year, he came second at a speed of 55.16 mph. He was to join HRD in 1925 and came fifth in the Junior TT that year.

George Grinton with his AJS machine at the 1922 Isle of Man TT in which he came second. He was later to ride for Norton.

Charlie Hough on his 1923 AJS for the Junior TT. In 1924, Hough was the first AJS rider across the line in the Senior TT, coming sixth. The following year, he came home fourth in the Junior TT, but failed to finish in the Senior TT. In 1926, he was seventh in the Junior TT, and in 1927, he came in eleventh in the Senior. Another notable success for Hough and his AJS was second place in the 1927 Ulster Grand Prix, which featured one of the first mass starts.

The AJS team for the 1923 Isle of Man TT Races. From the left, back row: Joe Stevens Jnr (Company Production Engineer), Arthur Barnett, -?-, -?-, H. F. Harris (rider), Bob Shakespeare, J. W. Hollowell (rider), Jimmy Simpson (rider on bike), Arthur Curran, G. Kelly (rider), George Rowley (rider), Charlie Hough (rider). Front row: Frank Longman (rider), Clarrie Wise (rider, more successful in trials riding), Hanford Stevens (rider kneeling), Len Cohen (rider), Arthur Cohen, Ossie Wade (rider).

Only two of the nine AJS riders entered finished the course, Harris in second place and Frank Longman in sixth. Billy Hollowell was to become engaged to George Stevens daughter, Millie. After coming second in the French Grand Prix of 1925, he was on the fifth lap of the Belgian Grand Prix when he crashed and was killed, a great blow to the Stevens Family.

George Rowley became one of the greatest AJS riders, especially in the Senior TT, where he came sixth in 1926, second in 1928, and was usually the only AJS top-ten finisher in the early 1930s. Frank Longman came second in the Senior TT in 1925 and third in 1926.

RUGBY

Despite being one of the oldest sports clubs in the town, founded in 1875, two years before the football team, Wolverhampton Rugby Club has not achieved the same national, or even regional, esteem as such as Moseley, Coventry, or even Dudley-Kingswinford. Even in the days before professionalism and the national league table system, they were never one of the game's powerhouses. They did manage to come top of the Mercia Order of Merit in 1981/82, despite being matched against such clubs as Worcester and Dudley-Kingswinford. Nowadays, they remain a traditional, friendly rugby club with a thriving junior system, operating from their traditional home in Castlecroft.

A number of eminent players have nevertheless emerged from the town, though not all of them played for the town's main club. Martin Cooper was first chosen for an England trial while still a Wolverhampton player, but was immediately snapped up by Moseley, and eventually won 11 international caps at fly half. Sam Doble, born in Red Lion Street, the son of a Wolverhampton policeman, played for Wolverhampton Tech before going on to play for his college at Cheltenham, and then Moseley, and in 1971-72 achieved the highest ever points total in a season, a total of 581 points, eventually beaten by Dusty Hare. After three caps for England, he joined the team's threatened boycott of the game in Ireland, because of the Troubles, and was the only one who did not back down, refusing to go for the sake of his family. He never played for England again. His brother Gordon Doble did play for Wolverhampton, becoming captain in 1979, and is still with the club, as a coach.

Above: Sam Doble, who was born in Red Lion Street, Wolverhampton, in March 1944, and who set the points scoring record of 581 points in a season playing for Moseley in 1971/72. Sam never played for Wolverhampton Rugby Club, as his brother did for many years. He began playing for Wolverhampton Technical College, and then for St Paul's Teacher Training College, Cheltenham. Word quickly spread that there was a versatile rugby player in the Cheltenham backwater who scored over 1,000 points in a year, and in 1965-66, he was recruited by both Staffordshire and Moseley, and became a point-scoring machine at full back. He played for his county for eight seasons, invariably being the top points scorer. In the year they won the county championship, 1969/70, he scored 65 of their total of 95 points.

The Wolverhampton Rugby Club 1969/70 team. Second left on the back row is Martin Cooper, who was picked for an England trial while still playing at Castlecroft. He was immediately recruited by Moseley. The first of his 11 England caps was against France in 1973. He scored just the one try for his country, giving him a total of only 4 points scored, not being the designated goal kicker. J. Pandya on the front row is the father of Steffan Pandya, the National Junior Badminton Champion in 1989 and 1990, with one full England cap in 1990.

Left to right, back row: M. Parr, M. Cooper, J. Owen, A. Moor, D. Folkes, A. Wade, I. Creed, R. Bracey. Front row, P. Miles, J. Hickman, J. Pandya, A. Hill (capt.), L. Harding, P. Rutherford, A. Rutherford.

Merit Table Winners ~ 1981/82

The WRC First VX squad in season 1981/82, when they came top of the Mercia medal table, above such notable clubs as Worcester and Dudley-Kingswindford. They are posing in front of the stand which used to grace the club's Castlecroft ground. On the right-hand end of the back row is Grahame Smith, who represented England at Under-21 level and then found a Scottish grandfather, so that he could become a Scotland B International. Fifth from the left on the back row is Gordon Doble, Sam Doble's brother, and while this book is being written, he is still playing for WRC.

Left to right, back row: J. Sherratt, A. Freeth, S. Parr, I. Day, G. Doble, C. Hart, W. Farman, R. Wainwright, A. Wood, G. Smith. Front row: R. Banks, S. Gabourel, W. Tranter, G. Singleton (capt.), N. Parr, G. Low, D. Cook.

Opposite below: Sam Doble forcing his way over for a try at the Reddings, one of 72 he scored for Moseley. In five successive seasons from 1967 to 1972, he was the highest points scorer in British Rugby and was particularly famous for the length of some of his penalty kicks. In 1972, he was taken on tour by England to South Africa, and in the single Test scored a conversion and four penalty goals in a famous 18-9 victory. He won two further caps in a 9 v 0 defeat against New Zealand and 25 v 6 defeat to Wales, in which he scored the two penalties. Despite scoring 20 out of England's total of 24 points during his three internationals, he was never to play for his country again. Because of the Troubles, the players threatened a boycott of the match in Dublin, and independent of mind, Sam was the only one not to back down, putting his family's concerns uppermost. Sam scored a record career total of 3,651 points in all first-class matches. Forced to retire when diagnosed with cancer in 1976, Sam died on 17 September 1977. A record-breaking rugby player, probably the best ever born in Wolverhampton, loved by everyone who knew him, it is strange that he is not included in the city's Sporting Hall of Fame.

England international, Nick Jeavons, only tentatively a Wolverhampton Sporting hero, as he was born in Calcutta, India, and never played for Wolverhampton Rugby Club, though he is now a member. He did play for the Wulfrun Rugby Club before going on to Moseley and gaining 14 caps for England as a flanker, from 1981 to 1983, in successive internationals. He scored just 4 points for his country, with just the one try.

RACQUET SPORTS

Wolverhampton has a strong base of racquet clubs, the most prominent being Wolverhampton Lawn Tennis & Squash Club. A number of our sporting heroes came out of this club, including squash player Anna Bullock and tennis player Susan Partridge. The club was founded in 1885, playing in St Marks' Road, but moving to its current location in Newbridge in 1935.

Another major tennis club in the area, with a fine junior section, is Albert Lawn Tennis Club, which was formed in 1921 out of the Clyno Sports Club in Albert Road, which had folded. The following year, they bought a site off Aldersley Road and a wooden army hut from Cannock Chase to use as a pavilion. All the courts were grass to begin with, though they are now AstroTurf, and in a slightly different area. The Albert was slightly quicker to get rid of their old wooden pavilion, compared to the Cricket Club just up the hill at Danescourt; the fine new brick pavilion was opened in 1998.

There are other tennis clubs in the city: Bilston, Hanbury, Tettenhall, Woodfield, Linden Lea, and Wombourne.

The Reverend John Thorneycroft Hartley holds the distinction of being the only Wimbledon champion from Wolverhampton, winning the third and fourth championships held at the All England tennis club. In 1879, Hartley defeated Irishman Vere St Leger Gould in the final in straight sets, while needing four sets to overcome Herbert Lawford in 1880. Hartley was born in Wolverhampton and was the grandson of George Benjamin Thorneycroft, the first mayor of Wolverhampton, and owner of the Shrubbery Ironworks in Horseley Fields. Hartley became a Church of England vicar and had a parish in North Yorkshire. In 1881, the quarter-finals were on a Friday, with the semi-finals scheduled for the Monday. Hartley went home by train on Saturday to take his church services the following day. He had to stay with a dying parishioner until the early hours of Monday morning, after which he rode his horse to Thirsk Station, took the train to King's Cross, and then a horse-drawn cab to Wimbeldon, changing in the cab. Luckily, his semi-final was held up by rain, allowing him to get some rest, and he made it to the final the following day, where he won 6-4 6-4 6-3. Hartley made the final a third time, in 1881, when he lost 6-0 6-1 to W. C. Renshaw, who went on to win a total of seven Wimbledon titles, a feat only equalled by Pete Sampras.

Susan Partridge was a tennis player who reached the fourth round of Wimbledon in 1952. Partridge was a member of Wolverhampton Lawn Tennis & Squash Club and held two match points in that fourth round clash against Maureen Connolly, in which she nearly prevailed with a tactical game, avoiding Little Mo's powerful backhand, and taking the pace off the ball. Connolly went on to win the event as well as the next five Grand Slams. Partridge won the Wimbledon junior singles title in 1948 and played for Great Britain in the Wightman Cup. She was a quarter-finalist in the 1953 French Open, and married a member of the French Davis Cup Team, Philippe Chatrier.

Anna Bullock was a leading British squash player and a member of Wolverhampton Lawn Tennis & Squash Club. Bullock was ranked number one in Britain from 1965 to 1968 and played for Great Britain in 15 internationals. Bullock was a multi-talented sportswoman, representing her Staffordshire in tennis, golf and hockey, and currently lives in Stone.

The Staffordshire Premier One winners of 1981, Albert Lawn Tennis Club. Among them is former Wimbledon player, Ted Beards. From left to right, top row: Ted Beards, John Pearce, Roger Moore. Bottom row: Alan Spencer, Jim Goodman, Bob Fearn (chairman), Graham Carter and Cliff Jones. Beards played in The Wimbledon Championships twice, losing in the first round to multi-Grand Slam winner Ken Rosewell as well as Tony Roach, who also won a Grand Slam and went on to coach, among others, Roger Federer.

Ted Beards won the Staffordshire Men's Singles title an incredible fifteen times from 1959 to 1982, the first thirteen when he was with Bilston Tennis Club, including ten in a row. As well as this, he won eleven Staffordshire Doubles titles with a variety of partners.

Beards was a teacher and became the unpaid coach at the Newbridge Club, but left when the club decided to hire a professional coach. Beards only learnt of this when the new man came down and introduced himself as the new professional coach, so Ted decided to pack his bags and coach at nearby Albert Lawn Tennis Club! Beards was a member of the Albert side that won the Staffordshire Premier One title in 1981, 1983 and 1984 and was runner-up in 1982 (suffering a shock last-day defeat to already relegated Bilston).

FOOTBALL

Wolverhampton Wanderers FC is the football club that represents the city of Wolverhampton. It has had a long and notable history, which includes three league championships and being at the forefront of the start of floodlit European football.

Wolves, as they are known, began as St Luke's FC in 1877 before becoming Wolverhampton Wanderers in 1879, when they merged with a football and cricket team called the Wanderers. St Luke's were formed by a group of school children from St Luke's school in Blakenhall.

After using local fields in their earliest years, Wolves moved to their current home of Molineux in 1889. Molineux is located in the heart of the city, just a stone's throw away from the city centre, meaning the club is embraced as an important part of the community. Outside the ground, there are statues of legendary Wolves player Billy Wright and player/manager Stan Cullis.

Wolves were one of the twelve founding members of the Football League in 1888, and in that season were beaten in the FA Cup final by 'the invincibles' of Preston North End. Wolves did go on to win the FA Cup in 1893 and 1908, and later on in 1948 and 1960.

Wolves came to international prominence in the 1950s with their three league titles and their floodlit friendlies against strong European opposition, culminating in them beating the powerful Hungarian side Honved 3-2, a match which was screened on national television and which prompted calls for what eventually became the European Cup.

The club has had a rollercoaster ride since, with two League Cup triumphs in 1974 and 1980 and a final place at the UEFA Cup in 1972 being followed by relegation to the Fourth Division in the 1980s. A Steve Bull-led resurgence saw Wolves regain a position in the second tier, and in 2003, they were finally promoted to the Premiership. Relegation immediately followed but they found themselves back in the top flight after winning the Championship in 2009.

Wolves at the moment sit in fourth place in the all-time Football League table, and hold records such as being the only club to win five separate divisional titles and being the only club to win the all-time domestic cup treble of the FA Cup, League Cup and Football League Trophy.

Above: The Wolves team of 1883/84 with the Wrekin Cup, their first trophy. Left to right, back row: A. Blackham, H. Dallard (umpire), T. Cliff, J. Baynton, C. Mason, J. Brodie (captain), E. Hadley, J. Griffiths. Front row: I. Griffiths, A. Lowder, A. Davidson, A. Pearson.

The 1908 Wolves FA Cup-winning team. Left to right, top row: Kenneth Hunt, Jack Jones, Billy Wooldridge (captain), Tommy Lunn, Ted Collins, Alf Bishop. Bottom row: Billy Harrison, Jack Shelton, George Hedley, Wally Radford, Jack Pedley. Before the game, their opponents Newcastle United felt so sure they would win they asked to pose with the cup beforehand, a request that was declined. There seemed to be some justification in their beliefs, as Wolves were at the time in the Second Division and Newcastle were the First Division champions but Wolves won 3-1 with goals from Hunt, Hedley and Harrison. Hunt was perhaps the most famous player, also winning an Olympic gold medal, representing Great Britain with an English National Amateur Team.

Opposite below: The Wolves team of 1907/08. Left to right, back row: E. Shepherd, W. Wooldridge, J. Jones, K. Hunt, J. Addenbrooke (secretary), T. Lunn, L. Lloyd, A. J. Evans. Middle row: W. Ward, G. Hedley, J. H. Jones, C. Radford, J. Pedley. Front row: A. Bishop, L. Collins, J. Shelton.

Jack Addenbrooke had been a St Luke's pupil, and was made secretary of the school team when only ten. After becoming a teacher, he rejoined the Wolves in 1883 as a reserve and, two years later, became secretary/manager, a post he held for an incredible thirty-seven years, the longest in the club's history. Even Alex Ferguson has not approached that sort of longevity.

Jackery Jones (on the back row) made 336 appearances for Wolves as a full back, and was to carry his cup-winners medal wherever he went. He was elected to the club's Hall of Fame in 2008.

The Dudley Road School League C winners in 1937. The captain, in the centre with the ball, is Arthur Rowley, who went on to become the Football League's all-time top scorer with an astonishing 434 goals in 619 appearances, spread over nineteen seasons and all four divisions. Born in Wolverhampton, Arthur only played for the Wolves during one season in the war, making 8 guest appearances and scoring 3 goals. His first club was West Brom; he then played for Fulham, Leicester and Shrewsbury. His elder brother, Jack, became one of Manchester United's all-time greats, scoring 208 goals for them in 422 appearances, and getting six England caps. Jack also played for the Wolves, during wartime games, when teams often fielded 'guest players', usually when they were home on leave, or stationed at military establishments nearby. He played just 8 times for the Wolves over five seasons during the war, but scored an astonishing 17 goals, including five in an 11-1 defeat of Everton and all eight in an 8-1 defeat of Derby! Even the great Steve Bull would not come close to such scoring feats.

Stan Cullis leads out Wolves for another game at Molineux. Cullis was an incredible servant for the club, being attached to the club for the best part of thirty years as a player and as a manager. His playing years were undoubtedly cut short by the Second World War and then injury, but he made 171 appearances for the club, including twice captaining the team as runners-up in the First Division. He also won twelve full caps for England on top of appearing in 20 wartime internationals. It was as a manager that Cullis flourished the most, managing Wolves in by far their most successful period, winning the First Division three times in 1954, 1958 and 1959 and the FA Cup in 1949 and 1960. Wolves were startlingly consistent under Cullis, finishing in the top three in the league in nine of his sixteen seasons in charge, but they started to decline at the end of his reign and he was sacked in 1964.

Above: The FA Cup-winning side of 1949. Under manager Stan Cullis and captain Billy Wright, this trophy was the first step of Wolves becoming one of the dominant forces in league football. Left to right, back row: Billy Crook, Roy Pritchard, Bert Williams, Bill Shorthouse, Terry Springthorpe. Front row: Johnny Hancocks, Sam Smyth, Stan Cullis, Billy Wright, Jesse Pye, Jimmy Dunn and Jimmy Mullen.

Left: Billy Wright holding the League Championship aloft in 1954. Born in Ironbridge, Shropshire, Wright was, after twenty years of service as a player, an iconic figure at Molineux, where he made 541 appearances and won three league championships as captain in 1954, 1958 and 1959 and one FA Cup in 1949. Wright was also Footballer of the Year in 1952 and holds the distinction of never being booked or sent off by a referee.

Above: England team with three Wolves players. Billy Wright is in the centre at the bottom and Bert Williams is the goalkeeper. Johnny Hancocks, winning one of his three England caps, is on the right-hand end of the back row, just about visible. Being only 5 feet 4 inches (with incredibly small size 2 feet), he should really have been allowed to sit on the front row. He and Jimmy Mullen would have played many more times on the wings for England, but for the presence of Tom Finney and Stanley Matthews. Born in Oakengates and bought from Walsall in 1946, he made 378 appearances for Wolves and scored 168 goals, those tiny feet possessing one of the hardest shots in the game.

Right: Bert Williams was the Wolves goalkeeper for twelve years, making 420 appearances, and won the FA Cup and the League Championship with the club in 1949 and 1954 respectively. Williams was also an England international, collecting twenty-four caps, including being first choice at the 1950 World Cup. Williams was born in Wolverhampton in Bradley, Bilston. After retirement, Williams was one of many players who went on to own a sports shop, Williams' in Bilston.

Stan Cullis with his 1957/58 Championship-winning squad. Malcolm Finlayson, Eddie, Stuart, Gerry Harris, Eddie Clamp, Billy Wright, Ron Flowers/Bill Slater, Norman Deeley, Peter Broadbent, Murray, Dennis Wilshaw/Bobby Mason/Colin Booth, Jimmy Mullen. This was the second title-winning squad under manager Stan Cullis.

Jimmy Mullen was quite simply one of the most talented and devoted players Wolves has ever seen, the one-club man serving as a player from 1947 to 1960, meaning he oversaw the whole of Wolves' most successful period. Comparisons could be drawn with Ryan Giggs, another devastating left winger who will next season enter his twentieth season as a Manchester United player. Mullen amassed 486 appearances and scored 112 goals for Wolves, a total which would surely have been much higher but for the Second World War. Mullen won twelve caps for England, scoring 6 times, and played in both the 1950 and 1954 World Cups. After retirement, Mullen ran a sports shop in Wolverhampton and died in 1987, aged sixty-four.

A twenty-one-year-old Ron Flowers in 1955 being coached by the legendary Wolves' trainer, Joe Gardiner. Joe joined Wolves as a seventeen-year-old in 1932, and made nearly 200 appearances for the club, mostly as a defender. He retired from playing in 1944 and became the club's trainer throughout the glory years until 1964, when he followed Stan Cullis to Birmingham City. Many supporters will remember him rushing to the aid of an injured player with a bucket of water and a 'magic sponge', with the smelling salts in his pocket for more serious injuries.

Flowers was a reserve throughout the England 1966 World Cup campaign. He had played in the 1962 World Cup in Chile, and ended up as England's top scorer, with two goals. Flowers spent fifteen years at Molineux and made 49 appearances in all for England. Flowers made 515 appearances for Wolves and was a member of all three League Championship-winning teams of the 1950s, as well as the FA Cup triumph of 1960. Ron Flowers left Wolves in 1967 and spent two years at Northampton Town, the second as player-coach. He then managed Telford United and took them to an FA Trophy Final at Wembley, before concentrating on running his sports shop in Queen's Street, Wolverhampton.

Above: Billy Wright leading out England on his hundredth cap, the first player from any country to reach that milestone. Behind him are Peter Broadbent, Ron Flowers, and Tommy Docherty (later a Wolves manager). Wright appeared in England's first three World Cup campaigns, in 1950, 1954 and 1958. He reached a total of 105 caps, and in the days before substitutes, started and finished every match. Wright is still the fifth-highest-capped player for England, and may have been higher had it not been for the Second World War.

Left: Peter Broadbent. Many of the fans who saw him play claim that he was the finest player ever to pull on the gold and black, and it was a crime that he only ever played for England seven times, the way to further caps being blocked by the selectors preference for Johnny Haynes. His seven England caps did include a match at the 1958 World Cup. The inside-right made 497 appearances for Wolves in thirteen years at the club, scoring 145 goals, and he was part of the club's three league championship-winning sides and the FA Cup winners of 1960.

Bill Slater holding aloft the FA Cup at Wembley in 1960, a year where he was also voted Footballer of the Year. Slater was another member of the team of the late 1950s early 1960s that was so successful. He started his career at inside forward before moving into defence. Slater was known for his composure and his distribution of the ball and played for Great Britain in the 1952 Olympics just before he joined Wolves and then went on to win twelve England caps while at the club.

The Wolves team in 1968, their first back in the big time, after two years in the second division. A season when they finished seventeenth, and the last complete season under Ronnie Allen, who was sacked after another poor start to the next campaign.

Left to right, back row: Stewart Ross, John Holsgrove, Dave Woodfield, Phil Parkes, Les Wilson, Derek Parkin, Mike Bailey. Front row: Dave Wagstaffe, Mike Kenning, Peter Knowles, Derek Dougan, Frank Wignall.

Peter Knowles, as every Wolves fan of the era knows, might have become the greatest player ever to pull on the Wolves shirt. Scoring 61 goals in 174 league appearances for the club, he was a mercurial inside forward, who would surely have gone on to greater things than his four England Under-23 caps, but he could not reconcile his religious beliefs with his volatile temperament on the pitch, and retired from the game aged just twenty-four. Wolves maintained his registration until all hope for a change of heart had gone.

John Richards and Derek Dougan. Richards scored 194 goals in a fourteen-year spell for the club, including the winner in the 1974 League Cup final, a club record until Steve Bull overtook it. He also won another League Cup in 1980, as well as a Second Division championship in 1977 and won a UEFA Cup runners-up medal in 1972. Despite his club form, Richards only won a solitary England cap against Ireland in 1973. Dougan scored 123 goals for the club in an eight-year spell, where he won 1974 League Cup and the Second Division championship in 1967. Dougan was capped forty-three times for Northern Ireland in his career.

Captain Mike Bailey holding aloft the League Cup after the 1974 victory. Bailey joined Wolves in 1966 and, in his first full season, helped Wolves to promotion. He helped the club establish itself in the top flight and was also part of the team that won the Texaco Cup on 1971 and reached the UEFA Cup final in 1972. In all, he made 436 appearances for the club in an eleven-year career.

The 1980 League Cup-winning team after victory over the European Champions, Nottingham Forest. Paul Bradshaw, Geoff Palmer, Derek Parkin, Peter Daniel, Emlyn Hughes (captain), George Berry, Kenny Hibbitt, Willie Carr, Andy Gray, John Richards, Mel Eves. Wolves won the match 1-0 with a goal from Gray, which meant a second League Cup triumph for the club in the space of seven years.

Perms, short shorts and chopper bikes: all redolent of the 1980s, five of the main stars of the Wolves team of the time. Left to right: Emlyn Hughes, Willie Carr, Andy Gray, Derek Parkin, John Richards. At the end of a hugely successful career forged at Liverpool, Hughes came to Wolves and was the captain of the 1980 League Cup-winning team. Hughes won three England caps while at Wolves, with fifty-nine others coming at Liverpool. Carr made 237 appearances for Wolves in a seven-year spell, where he won the Second Division championship and the League Cup. Gray moved to Wolves from Aston Villa for what was then a national record of £1.5 million. The striker scored 38 goals on 138 appearances for the club, including the winner in the 1980 League Cup final. Parkin holds the club record for appearances with an incredible 609 in a fourteen-year spell with the club, appearing in both League Cup finals and also in the Second Division Championship-winning side. He was once called up to the England squad but never played, but did win five U23 caps, perhaps because he always played left back for Wolves, though he was a right-footed player.

Steve Bull wheeling away after one of his club record 306 goals in 561 appearances for the club. Born in nearby Tipton, Bull was transferred from local rivals West Bromwich Albion in 1986 for a snipped price of £65,000, which also included Andy Thompson. Bull was the key player in the club's resurgence when they won back-to-back titles in the Fourth and then Third Division as well as the Sherpa Van Trophy, amazingly hitting the 50 goals mark in each season. These triumphs meant Wolves became the only club to win all four Football League divisional titles, as well as having won a Division Three South title. Despite this, he never achieved his goal of reaching the Premiership for Wolves, his only top-flight appearance coming with Albion in the old First Division. Bull was also a member of the 1990 England World Cup squad, who reached the semi-finals. Bull won 13 caps for his country and scored 4 goals, a remarkable achievement by a player from the lower divisions.

Graham Turner directing operations from scaffolding in front of the Waterloo Road Stand, showing just how decrepit the stadium had become after two of the stands were closed, because of the new safety regulations. Building the John Ireland Stand behind the old Molineux Street Stand, before knocking that down, had already destroyed the wonderful atmosphere that used to exist in the old Molineux. The pitch was moved over, and the new stand was not connected to the rest of the ground. In the old ground, the stands were right on the edge of the pitch, and the noise as Wolves kicked towards the old North Bank in the second half, seeking a winner, or an equaliser, was always worth a goal in itself. The decline of the stadium had echoed the decline on the pitch, and it was Graham Turner who brought about the revival of the club, not least with his audacious purchase of Steve Bull from Black Country rivals, Albion. The arrival of Sir Jack Hayward completed the job, as his money rebuilt the ground.

Graham Turner and his coaches holding the Sherpa Van Trophy after winning it at Wembley 2-0 against Burnley. It was a fitting celebration of the Football League's centenary, with two of the league's founders competing in a cup final in front of a full-house of 80,000, perhaps more so than the league's actual celebrations a few weeks later. Though the Sherpa Van Trophy was something of a step down for such fine old clubs, they were both grateful to be back at Wembley after a long break. It's often overlooked that Wolves also actually won a Sherpa Van, a large minibus to transport players to the training ground.

Graham Turner and Steve Bull holding the Third Division Championship Trophy. This marked Wolves' second successive promotion under the guidance of Turner as the club reached the Second Division. Turner joined Wolves in 1986 and, as manager, turned around the club, who were then languishing in the Fourth Division, moving them up to the second tier. He left the club, however, after a series of failed promotion attempts under new chairman Sir Jack Hayward.

The Championship Trophy returns to Molineux, albeit for winning the second tier of English football. Visible from left to right: Dave Edwards, Christophe Berra, Stephen Ward, Wayne Hennessey, Karl Henry, Sylvain Ebanks-Blake, Jody Craddock, Richard Stearman, Matt Jarvis. Wolves secured top place in the league in the penultimate match after topping the league for the majority of the season. Club captain Craddock and Henry, on-field captain for a chunk of the season, hold the trophy aloft, with key players including player of the season Kevin Foley and 25-goal top scorer Ebanks-Blake. Other regular players not included in the photo include Chris Iwelumo, Michael Kightly, David Jones, Neill Collins and Andy Keogh. Under manager Mick McCarthy, this promotion ensured only their second season in the top flight since 1984.

OTHER SPORTS

Wolverhampton Amateur Boxing Club was formed in 1937 on the initiative of Harry Dallard, a local coal-merchant, and the club's HQ was in the Goldthorn Social Club, Goldthorn Hill. After the war, the training room was initially upstairs in St George's Hall, and then the Rose & Crown in Blakenhall. There were other boxing clubs in the town at the time: Windmill, Pennfields, The Scotlands, Bilston Golden Gloves, and Wednesfield, and the Central Boys Club also incorporated boxing. WABC moved to Montrose Street, and then, after a fire, to Union Street.

As well as Midland and National ABA champions, the club produced two Olympians, Roy Addison, in the 1960 Olympics in Rome, and Tony Wilson, in the 1984 Olympics in Los Angeles, where he reached the quarter-finals. Wilson then turned professional and became British Light-Heavyweight Champion.

WABC continued to have a nomadic existence until they finally settled on their current premises in Colliery Road in 2005. The former Willenhall Road school building was in a terrible state, having been disused for a long while and flooded when the council let the club have it. A huge amount of work eventually saw a fine headquarters for all amateur boxing in Wolverhampton. Any training night will reveal a host of youngsters learning the disciplines and art of boxing, alongside prospects for future glory.

As one of only a handful of boxing clubs in the country to have an Olympic-size ring, it is set to host a number of boxing teams for the 2012 Olympics, with the Jamaicans the first to sign up.

Tony Wilson, Wolverhampton-born light-heavyweight champion, preparing to start a bout in an East German tournament in 1984, in which he won a bronze medal. He had joined Bilston Golden Gloves Club in 1975, and became an ABA Junior silver medallist the following year. In 1978, he transferred to Wolverhampton Amateur Boxing Club, and Ray Green became his coach. He became Senior ABA Champion in 1983 and 1984, and was selected to represent Great Britain at the 1984 Los Angeles Olympics, where he reached the quarter-finals. He had been awarded the bout by the judges, guaranteeing him a bronze medal at least, but the decision was overturned by a special panel. The following year, he turned professional, after 82 amateur bouts and 67 wins, and in 1987, he became British Light-Heavyweight Champion, going on to defend it twice to win a Lonsdale Belt outright. He retired in 1990 with a professional record of 28 fights, 20 wins and a draw. Perhaps his most famous fight was against Steve McCarthy in September 1989. When Tony was knocked down by McCarthy, his mother, Minna climbed into the ring and began hitting McCarthy with her shoe. She drew blood and McCarthy refused to continue, causing a riot when Wilson was awarded the fight on a TKO. Wilson has since worked as a personal trainer and fitness coach.

The senior golf club in Wolverhampton is the South Staffordshire golf club, which formed in 1892, using a course on Penn Common. They moved to the existing 160-acre course at Danescourt in 1908. Their most famous golfer is now the club's Director of Golf, Peter Baker.

The vacant Penn Common course was taken over by a new club, which formed in 1908, the Penn Golf Club, who had to put up with the livestock, which were still allowed to graze across the common, a situation which continued until they bought the freehold in 1955. Their most famous golfer, Charles Stowe, was actually born in a cottage on the common. He was a coalminer but, as an artisan member, quickly became an accomplished golfer and won countless championships. In 1935, he was summoned to play for England for the first time and, in 1938, was a member of the first Walker Cup team to beat the Americans. Three times he came second in major championships, the Amateur in 1948, and the English Championship in 1947 and 1949.

Peter Baker holding up the Credit Suisse Challenge Trophy which he won for the second time in 2009. Baker was born in Shifnal and learned to play on his father's nine-hole course at Himley Hall. He was a member of the Walker Cup Team in 1985 and turned professional the following year. He has competed in over 500 tournaments on the European Tour, winning three, and in 1993 was a member of the Ryder Cup Team at the Belfry. Though on the losing side, he personally won three points out of four.

Wolverhampton Hockey Club was founded in 1904, and is currently based within Fordhouses Cricket Club, using the AstroTurf pitches at Aldersley Stadium, just five minutes away. One of the most famous hockey players from the town is Rachel Heyhoe-Flint, who played in goal for England, but features elsewhere in this book, as she achieved even greater fame as a cricketer.

Charlotte Craddock, the youngest member of Great Britain's Hockey Team at the Beijing Olympics, aged just seventeen. Though born in Wolverhampton, she is a member of Cannock Hockey Club, the finest in the area, and made her debut for Great Britain against Argentina in November 2007, as a forward, just before Beijing, having never played for England. She had been a regular member of the Wolverhampton Cricket Club's Under-13 boys side, and could have progressed a long way in cricket, if she had chosen that over hockey.

Wolverhampton is blessed with a sporting facility of national importance in the Rifle Ranges at Aldersley, now named the Frank Spittle Rifle Ranges after something of a giant in the world of air rifle, small-bore and crossbow shooting, Wolverhampton-born Frank Spittle. Home Guard units continued to operate until 1957, and company teams continued to operate strong competitions. Wolverhampton was to dominate the inter-town league, winning this competition for the ninth time in a row in 1966. The outdoor range built at Aldersley was augmented with the new National Indoor Air Rifle Centre, which was opened in 1974.

Upper: Frank Spittle on the right, of the James Gibbons Rifle Team, who won the Midland United Shield. Frank took up competitive shooting during the war. Home Guard units, using rifle ranges built by local companies during the war, began competitive shooting after the war, and Frank was part of the 8th Battalion Team at West Park Drill Hall, which won the National Championship in the year the Home Guard stood down in 1957. Individually, he dropped only one point with a score of 1,399 out of 1,400. James Gibbons used an ex-army hut as their rifle range on the Birmingham New Road. In 1957, he achieved the status of World Master, and first became part of the England team in 1965 against Scotland.

Lower: John Spittle, son of Frank, who in 1969 became the first-ever British junior to win a medal abroad when he took silver in the European International Shooting Championships at Versailles, missing the gold by one point.

Wolverhampton's racecourse was originally the Broadmeadow, which was on the site of what is now West Park, and the first race recorded there was in 1825. When the council bought the course to develop into a park in 1878, a new course was laid out on the former estate of Dunstall Hall. The largely triangular course was named Dunstall Park, and has remained the city's racecourse ever since. Also used as the town's airport from 1910 to 1919, the racecourse remained very little changed until complete redevelopment in 1993, to become the country's first floodlit all-weather track.

Kevin Darley, born in Tettenhall, was British Flat Racing Champion Jockey in the year 2000. He had his first win at Haydock in 1977, the first of eleven wins that year. The following year, he was British Flat Race Champion Apprentice and became a steady winner through the 1980s. He broke the magic ton for the first time in 1993 with 143 winners, with over 100 wins following in each of the next four years. He became champion jockey in 2000, and was second, fourth, and third over the next three years, retiring in 2007.